Children's rooms

in a weekend

Children's rooms
in a weekend

Roo Ryde

MEREHURST

Acknowledgements

I dedicate this book to Mr Shoes, Pishi, Lobi, my sister and best friend Lisa, Mum and Dad for their loving support and patience with this project and for allowing me to clutter up their houses with all my bits and pieces; Dominic Blackmore for his brilliant photography, calm approach to everything and great lunches!; Anna Ryder-Richardson of Squidgy Things for her expert sewing skills and ability to keep laughing whatever time of day; Adrian and Albert for always being on hand to help me out; and Sara Colledge at Merehurst, who never failed to come up with a solution to the problems I encountered. Also a big thank you to everyboby else who was involved with this project and helped me to create the colourful results.

Please note that the projects in this book have been designed for the rooms of children, not for those of babies or young toddlers.

Reprinted 1998
First published 1996 by Merehurst Limited,
Ferry House, 51-57 Lacy Road, London, SW15 1PR

Copyright © 1996 Merehurst Limited

ISBN 1-85391-771-0

A catalogue record for this book is available from the British Library.

Editor: Geraldine Christy
Designer: Anthony Cohen
Photographer: Dominic Blackmore
Stylist: Roo Ryde
Artworks: Brihton Iliustration

Colour separation by Dot Gradations, England

Printed in Singapore by Tien Wah Press

Contents

Introduction *6*

Button pelmet and hold-backs *8*

Bow bed canopy *14*

Pom-pom chair and cushion *20*

'Fat cat' bean bag *26*

Sports peg rail and PVC kit bag *30*

Fabric-fronted shelf units *34*

'Daisy Daisy' noticeboard *38*

Noughts and crosses headboard game *42*

Eight-drawer chest *46*

Playing card curtains and tie-backs *52*

Elephant pocket storage system *56*

Porthole blackboard *60*

Painted and stamped toy chest *66*

Templates *70*

Glossary *76*

Suppliers *78*

Index *79*

Introduction

Although I am a firm believer in trying to create rooms for children that will grow with them, I also love to include as much colour, texture and as many elements of fun as possible. I have found that one can combine both these ideas and still produce a practical bedroom that can also stimulate thought and imagination in a child's mind.

Most parents start off with the best of intentions when their first child comes along, and take great pleasure in planning and decorating the baby's room. But as your first child grows up and maybe another one or two babies have arrived, in between trying to juggle a job and organize the whole family you might suddenly realize that your child's room does not offer the sort of stimuli and excitement that is needed. Bear in mind that a well-planned room with plenty of storage space and a work station will not only make life easier for your child but also for you. If your children are happy with their room they will be more content to play and do their homework in it and, perhaps, more willing to keep it tidy!

So let your creativity run wild and involve your children in the decisions and choices for their room – remember that at the end of the day you can close the door on it all while they are left alone to enjoy their own private fantasy land.

Great decorating ideas do not need to depend on spending a lot of money or on having beautifully proportioned rooms – anyway few of us have the ways or means of being able to live in the style that we all dream about. I have tried to be cost-conscious when planning all the projects in this book and often they include items that you may already have lying around the house. If not, they can be readily picked up on a low budget or second-hand.

I hope that you will enjoy making the projects that I have created for this book. Practical, easy-to-follow steps are provided for all of them and you need no special skills – just a

weekend! But do bear in mind that the projects are not designed for you to follow slavishly. If you prefer to adapt or interpret my designs to give different effects

then go ahead. Try to incorporate your children's favourite colours, favourite stories or cartoon characters, their sports and hobbies. Most of the projects are suitable for both boys and girls, but some of them may have a more feminine or masculine appeal. I hope that you will find all of them of use and that you can draw inspiration even from those that are not immediately appropriate for your children.

Since I have no formal design or dressmaking training I am inclined to think of myself as a 'layman's designer'. Many of the techniques that I have used for the projects are designed to save time and are based on experience. More often than not I try to combine steps, but if you feel more comfortable breaking some of the steps down into further stages do feel free to do so. The important point is to achieve a satisfactory end result.

I have tried to keep the instructions as clear and as uncomplicated as possible. Any points that need further explanation can be found in the tinted advice boxes that accompany the detailed steps to the projects.

You will notice that in many of the photographs that accompany the steps I have used mainly white cotton thread for sewing. This has been done so that it shows up well in the demonstrations – but when you machine or hand sew fabric do try and use a matching coloured cotton thread so that it is less visible.

I have tried to make all the projects in the book as colourful and eye-catching as possible. But besides looking great they all have a practical element to them – they are all well worth spending a weekend on. You may find some of the projects will take up most of your time over a weekend, while others can be completed much more quickly.

So go ahead and surprise your children with one of these wonderful weekend makes. I guarantee you that not only will they be grateful, but you will also be very proud of the end results.

Good luck.

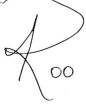

Button pelmet and hold-backs

A bright button theme provides a splash of colour that will enliven any window. Children love to choose the colours, so enlist their help to make the 'buttons'.

Windows come in all sorts of shapes and sizes, and deciding how to dress them without spoiling their shape always taxes my imagination. But an easy and effective solution is to 'create an illusion'. Dress a small window grandly and it suddenly takes on a new look. Hang curtains so that they cover part of a window that is disproportionately large for the room and the window seems smaller.

Irregularly shaped windows, especially in children's rooms, can be used to advantage and transformed into eye-catching features. There are no hard and fast rules to which you have to adhere. Kids love bright and bold rooms, so get them actively involved in deciding on the look.

The window that we have worked around here is an average-sized sash window. Creating the pelmet and hold-backs for it, with their button theme, brings in an element of fun. Once you have made your pelmet and hold-back bases you could turn them into whatever else takes your fancy – such as a flower theme, funny faces, or, if your child is mad about motor racing, for instance, steering wheels for the hold-backs and racing cars along the pelmet.

Day One

Step 1

Prepare all the wood pieces. Each hold-back requires a backplate, a piece of wooden dowelling and a front button plate. These need to be pre-drilled before priming. The back plates need a screw hole in each corner and one in the centre. The dowelling needs a screw hole in each end and the button needs a screw hole right in the centre. The four other holes on the button, for the laces, need to be drilled with an extra large drill bit.

Step 2

Using primer paint, paint all the pieces of wood to seal the surface. Then leave them to dry. When dry, using your chosen paint colour, paint all the pieces of wood and again leave to dry. Try to apply the paint with even strokes for a smooth colour finish.

Step 3

Screw the piece of dowelling into the backplate with a 4 cm (1½ in) long screw inserted from the base of the backplate.

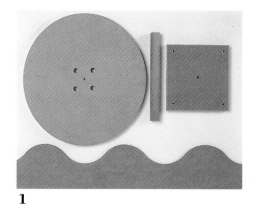

1

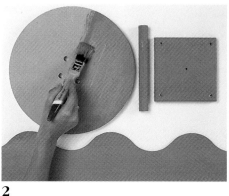

2

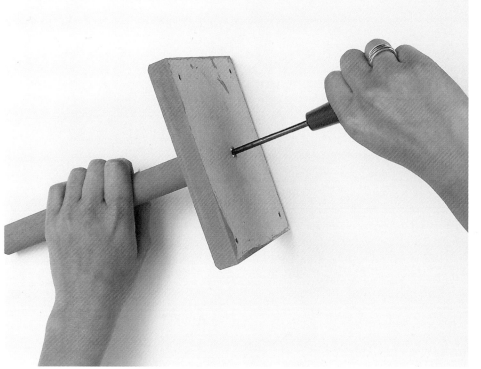

3

Cutting the pieces

If you have a jigsaw, then you may prefer to cut the MDF pieces yourself. Otherwise I would recommend that you get your local wood merchant to do it for you.

If you decide to use a jigsaw, draw a template for each shaped piece (button and pelmet) onto heavy brown paper. The button backplate can be measured and drawn straight onto your piece of MDF. Place the paper template onto the MDF and, using a pencil, trace around the outlines onto the wood.

Following the pencil lines, cut out the MDF shapes with the jigsaw. Use a proper workbench for sawing so that you can clamp the piece to be cut.

Day Two

Step 4

Using masking tape, mask off the first stage of the design on the button front. Measure and divide the face into five sections and mask them off leaving 1 cm (⅜ in) in between to paint. Using a contrasting paint colour, paint the lines and leave to dry. If you rest the button on top of a can of paint, it will make it a lot easier to work on.

Step 5

When the first set of lines are completely dry, repeat step 4, this time masking off the lines in the opposite direction. Paint and leave to dry.

Step 6

Using a bradawl through the screw holes, mark on the wall exactly where you want the hold-backs to be positioned. Drill these four holes and place a wall plug that matches the screw size into each hole. Then screw the backplate onto the wall.

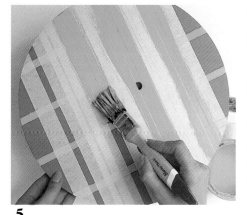

4

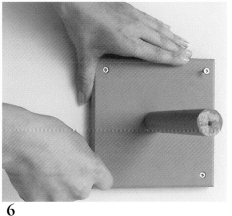

5

6

Painting wood

Although I might not always explain in detail in the steps, it is important that you prime all raw, never-before-painted surfaces. Beware of 'all-purpose' primer paints – buy one that is specifically designed for the type of surface on which you are working.

For all the projects in the book a white primer combined with an undercoat is the quickest option. For the top coat, unless otherwise instructed, choose an oil-based paint as this will leave you with a more durable surface.

Step 7

With the button front positioned centrally over the wooden dowelling, place a screw into the centre hole and screw the two pieces together. Use a small amount of filler to cover the head of the screw and disguise it. Then paint over it, and, when dry, thread the laces through the four holes.

Step 8

Once the completed hold-back is in position, drape the curtains behind it.

Step 9

Using a selection of different colours of modelling clay, roll out sausage shapes and cut these into fat discs. Gently roll these with a 'mini' rolling pin to flatten them. Create different designs by adding other coloured pieces or try rolling two colours together for a marbled effect. Make either two or four holes in each 'button', using a long, pointed implement. Place the clay 'buttons' on a baking tray and bake for the manufacturer's specified time, and then leave them to cool.

7

8

9

Using modelling clay

Modelling clay is an easy material to work with and is available in a large range of colours from craft and children's toy shops. It is a 'clean and dry' clay – you will not end up with a mess everywhere – and it is ideal for children to play with. Do follow the manufacturer's instructions on the packet when baking the clay. Baking it hardens the clay up and makes it very durable.

Step 10

Lay your piece of pelmet down and position the buttons in place until you are happy with the overall effect. Then, working from one end, glue them in place. Leave them to set before moving the pelmet. The pelmet should be attached to two brackets placed over the window for a really secure fixing. (See *Putting up the pelmet board*.)

Step 11

The finished pelmet in place. This decorative treatment will transform the plainest window or dullest room into something quite spectacular.

Putting up the pelmet board

Determine the location for the pelmet by aligning it with the window or ceiling. If they are not parallel, use a spirit level as a guide. Using the pelmet brackets, mark off the drilling points through the bracket fixing holes with a pencil. Drill the holes and push wall plugs into them. Screw in the brackets, and attach the pelmet to the brackets.

10

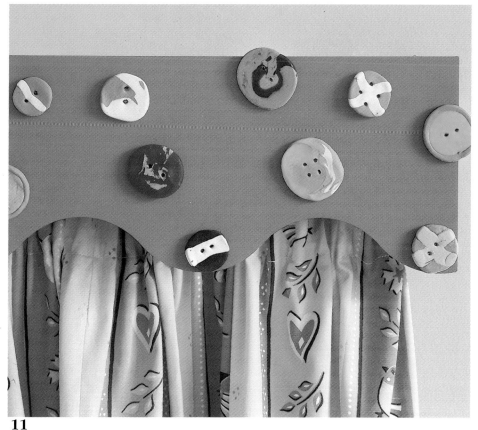

11

Bow bed canopy

A feminine and simple solution for a dull bedroom that will delight young ladies of all ages. This elegant bow theme has been followed through to create matching bow bedlinen.

Children seem to grow up much faster nowadays and from an early age they know exactly what they want – from the style of clothes they wear, and toys they choose, to the design of their rooms. But for girls who just want to be girls it is quick and easy to give their bedrooms a facelift with a few feminine touches.

This elegant bed canopy operates on a very simple principle. Once the rail has been attached to the wall you simply clip the fabric to the rings hanging from it. I bought about 10 m (11 yd) of cheap muslin and hemmed it at the top and bottom. With selvedges on each side of the muslin, I did not need to sew side seams. But what really made the canopy look extra special were the jumbo wadded bows that I used to tie back the muslin.

If you want to take the bow theme one step further you could cut out some strips of material from a coordinating fabric, neaten them up and then tie them into bows through the metal rings on the bed canopy rail. You could also add a matching fabric border all the way down the inside edges of the muslin canopy. I followed the bow theme through to the duvet cover and pillowcase. Both of these are very easy to make and both use the same method.

Planning your time

DAY ONE

AM: Cut out the two templates and all the fabric pieces

PM: Make the wadded bows

DAY TWO

AM: Make the pillowcases

PM: Make the duvet cover

Tools and materials

3 coordinating fabrics (see steps for amounts needed for individual items)

For each bow: 115 g (4 oz) wadding, measuring 40 x 25 cm (16 x 10 in)

For each bow: 25 cm (10 in) of satin ribbon 1 cm (⅜ in) wide

Thick paper for making the two templates

Scissors

1

Day One

Step 1

For each canopy bow tie you will need to cut out: two pieces of fabric 40 x 25 cm (16 x 10 in) and one piece of wadding the same size for the body of the bow; one piece of fabric 18 x 12 cm (7 x 5 in) for the centre loop; two fabric shapes following pattern A on page 70 (cut these on the double with the fold of the fabric along the 9 cm (3½ in) side so that you have long, narrow pieces for the bow tails); one piece of ribbon 25 cm (10 in) long.

Step 2

Place the bow body pieces right sides together, with the piece of wadding beneath them both. Machine sew this 'sandwich' all around the edge, leaving an opening about 12 cm (5 in) wide on one of the long sides. Push the pieces through the opening to turn the material the right way round, so that the wadding is now sandwiched in the middle (see page 55). Hand sew the opening.

Step 3

Place the two bow tail pieces made from pattern A right sides together. Machine sew all the way around, leaving an opening on one of the long sides. Turn the right way round and hand sew the opening. Iron flat.

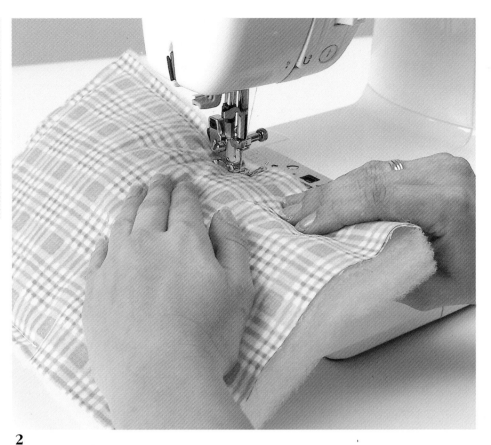

2

3

Step 4

Using a hot iron, press a 2 cm (¾ in) hem along each long side of the centre loop. Wrap the loop around the centre of the wadded bow body to form the bow shape, and hand sew the loop ends together.

Step 5

Feed the long bow tails through the centre loop that you have just sewn, so that the tails are of equal length. Then feed the ribbon through the loop in the same way. It is this ribbon that will secure the bow to the hold-back hook.

4

5

Making the duvet cover and pillowcases

The duvet cover and pillowcases are both made in the same way, although the steps describe how to make the pillowcase. Remember, however, when making up the duvet cover, that it has three pairs of ties along the bottom, not two pairs as for the pillowcase. To make the duvet cover you can use either an extra wide sheeting fabric or other easy-care material. For a single duvet cover the fabric must be 145 cm (58 in) wide.

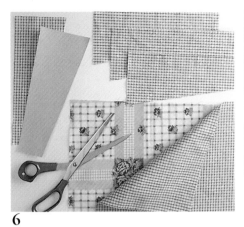

6

Day Two

Step 6

For the pillowcase cut two pieces of contrasting fabric 75 x 55 cm (30 x 22 in) and four fabric shapes following pattern B on page 70 (cut these on the double with the fold of the fabric along the 5 cm (2 in) side). For the duvet cover similarly cut two pieces of contrasting fabric 210 x 145 cm (84 x 58 in) and six fabric shapes following pattern B.

Step 7

Pair up all the ties, right sides together, and machine sew around them, leaving a small opening through which you can turn them the right way round. Then press them flat.

Step 8

Neaten the top and bottom edges of the opening of the pillowcase by placing them with the wrong side facing up and pressing in 1 cm (⅜ in) of fabric. Fold over a further 4 cm (1½ in) of fabric, press and then machine along the edge. Position both the ties on the folded hem for the pillowcase (but note there will be three ties for the duvet cover) and machine sew in place, one machine line at the base of the tail and one higher up near the edge.

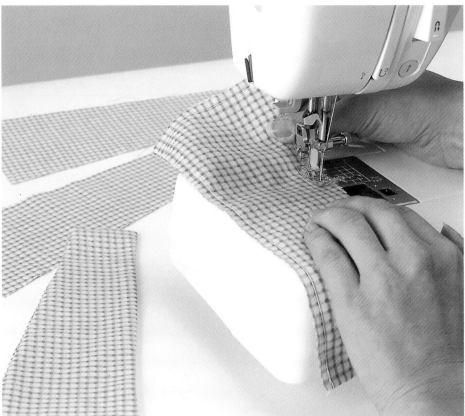

7

8

Step 9

To assemble the pillowcase, sew French seams on the remaining three sides. To do this, place the wrong sides of the fabric together, machine around the three 'closed' sides, then turn the pillowcase inside out, right sides together. Make sure that you have pulled out all the corners, then press flat along the seam lines. Then sew a second seam 1 cm (⅜ in) from the first (which is now the folded edge), enclosing the raw edges. Turn the right way round and press the seam allowance flat to one side of the seam

Step 10

Screw a tie-back hook into the wall each side of the bed, making sure that there is a good 15 cm (6 in) clearance from the bed edge. Using the ribbon on the back of the bow, tie it around the muslin drapes, pull them back and secure to the hook.

9

10

Pom-pom chair and cushion

Cheer up an old chair with a multitude of colours and a bright, comfortable cushion. Then paint other furniture in the room to match for a smart and fun look.

Most people have a plain wooden chair in their house somewhere. This project shows you how such an ordinary piece of furniture can be transformed into a unique and colourful child's chair that is sure to be treasured.

Look beyond the framework of the chair and see the possibilities for creativity. The simple wooden chair described here looked completely different once it had been painted, and with the addition of some fun wooden balls screwed into the top of the chair frame. Continuing the theme I designed a cushion for the chair decorated with colourful balls and trimmed with coordinating pom-pom trimming.

The theme then extended to a small round occasional table, which was given a new lease of life using the same paint colours and decorated with the 'ball' design. Even the curtain in the room ties in with the scheme, with the addition of its pom-pom trimming.

Be adventurous with your choice of colours, but do give them a test run first to make sure that they all sit comfortably together. Once you are happy with your colour combinations you will find all sorts of pieces that you can paint.

Planning your time

DAY ONE
AM: Sand chair and wash it down
Paint one colour

PM: Paint other colours

DAY TWO
AM: Cut out cushion and design

PM: Sew cushion

Tools and materials

Plain wooden chair

Fine-grade sandpaper

All-in-one white primer and undercoat

Satin-finish coloured paints

Paintbrushes

Fabric for cushion base

Cushion pad

Fabric for design on cushion

Trimming

Scissors

Masking tape

2 round wooden door knobs (optional if the chair is for a young child)

2 double-ended screws

Day One

Step 1

Choose three or four paint colours for the chair and cushion trimmings to match them. Two wooden door knobs complete the chair.

Step 2

Using fine-grade sandpaper, gently rub down the chair all over to provide a good 'key' for your primer and paint. If you are going to add wooden balls, drill holes in the top of the frame and in the knobs. When you have finished sanding, use a damp cloth to wipe the chair down.

Step 3

After priming the chair, decide which colours to paint different parts of the chair and use masking tape to mask off any adjoining edges while you paint each colour. Paint the two wooden door knobs.

1

2

3

Priming the chair

Although it is not shown in the steps, it is important that you prime all raw, never-before-painted surfaces (see page 11). For the wooden chair I used an all-in-one white primer and undercoat. For the top coat I chose a satin-finish oil-based paint as this gives a more durable surface.

Day Two

Step 4

When the chair and knobs are dry screw the knobs into place on each side of the chair frame using a double-ended screw. The chair can be varnished to protect the paint finish. I recommend that you varnish any item that is going to be placed in a child's bedroom so that it can withstand wear and tear. General-purpose oil-based varnishes and polyurethane varnish are the toughest wearing and most waterproof.

Step 5

Cut out two pieces of fabric 42 x 42 cm (17 x 17 in) for the cushion cover and two circles 8 cm (3 in) in diameter for each circle to be sewn on. You will also need 160 cm (64 in) of your chosen trimmings.

Step 6

Place the fabric circles right sides together and machine sew them all the way round. Make a small slit in the centre on one side, nick around all the edges and then turn the circle through so that it is the right way round. Lightly press with an iron.

4

5

6

Fixing the knobs with double-ended screws

Wooden door knobs are available in a variety of shapes, and adding them to the chair gives a special touch. If they are not pre-drilled, it will be necessary to drill a hole into them and a corresponding one into the chair where you want to fix them. Connect them together with a double-ended screw. This looks similar to a screw with no head and must be the same size as the holes you drill.

Step 7

Pin on all the circles in the desired positions on the top piece of your cushion. Then machine sew them all around their edges.

Step 8

Working on the right side of the top piece of the cushion, machine sew the pom-pom trimmings all the way round.

Step 9

Place the bottom piece of the cushion with the top piece, right sides together. Machine sew around three sides and halfway down the fourth one, making sure to sew right on the edge of the trimming braiding.

7

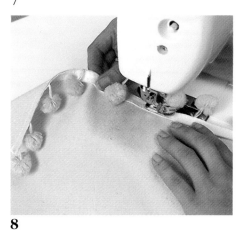

8

9

Choosing trimmings

If you cannot match up the colours for your trimmings, look out for inexpensive ones and dye them yourself. The pom-poms that I used were dyed using cold water dyes to match the colours of the fabric appliqué shapes. Cold water dyeing is quick and easy to do. Simply dissolve the dye and dye fix in the stated amount of water, following the manufacturer's recommended guidelines, and submerge the trimmings. Check every ten minutes until the trimmings have the depth of colour that you require. Remove, rinse and hang up until dry.

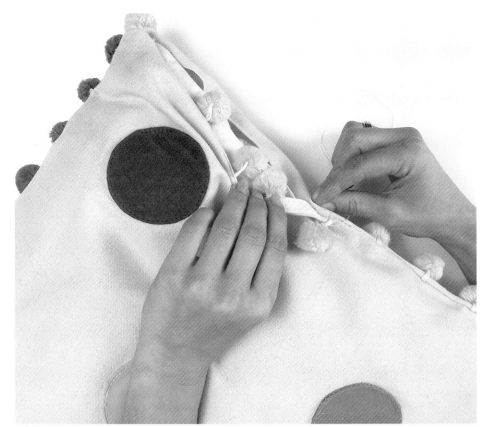

10

Step 10
Turn your cushion cover the right way round and put your cushion pad inside. Hand sew the opening.

Step 11
The completed cushion with fabric circles and trimmings to match the chair. Once you have mastered the methods involved in making this cushion, why not try designing your own, using different shapes and fabrics, or make a reversible cushion that has an interesting detail on both sides.

Hand sewing openings

Where openings or seams must be sewn up by hand from the right side of the fabric use a slipstitch. To do this take the needle across the opening and make a small stitch 2 mm (⅛ in) long along one side of the opening, then take the needle across the opening and make a similar stitch on the other side, closing the two sides together. Continue to the end and then fasten the thread off in the seam.

11

'Fat cat' bean bag

Floor seating is always popular with children and this cat will soon become a well-loved friend. Adapt the idea to make other animal bean bags.

Planning your time

DAY ONE
AM: Cut out all the pieces

PM: Machine sew the
face together

DAY TWO
AM: Machine sew the paws
together

PM: Assemble the cat

Tools and materials

Dark heavy-duty fabric

Two contrasting fabrics

**55 g (2 oz) wadding for the tail
(you can also add wadding to the
face and paws)**

Polystyrene balls

Pinking shears

Scissors

Thick brown paper for template

Not only lovable but also practical, this cuddly fat cat is comfortable to sit on. Its body and head are filled with polystyrene balls, which are available from the haberdashery or craft departments of major stores. Like many of the projects in this book, 'Fat Cat' is very easy to adapt to other shapes and sizes. Whatever animal bean bag that your children want or whatever colours coordinate best with their room, as long as you follow the same basic steps, you can cut out and make a whole host of different animals.

For the base of the animal's body choose a fairly dark colour and make sure that it is a heavyweight, durable fabric, as this part will receive the most wear and tear. For the 'additions' that turned the bag into a cat I used a mixture of felt and cotton drill.

You may wish to make the outer cover removable and washable. To do this, cut out a second head and body shape, about 3 cm (1¼ in) smaller all the way round. Use this as an inner lining, machine sewing it all the way round and leaving a gap to put the polystyrene balls into. Then fill this inner body with the balls and hand sew to close the opening. This body can then be stuffed inside the 'real' animal, and the base of the outer animal secured with Velcro or press studs.

1

2

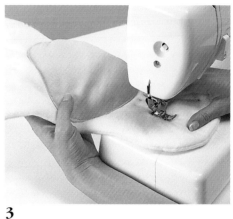

3

4

Day One

Step 1

Enlarge the templates on page 71 to the size you require and trace around them on brown paper to make your own templates. The body of the cat I made measured 118 cm (48 in) from head to base and 75 cm (30 in) across the width. Use your enlarged templates to cut out all the pieces, using pinking shears for the body pieces. Cut two pieces for the body, head and ears from one piece of black fabric; one black base circle with its diameter the same as the body base (in this case 75 cm [30 in]); two black tail pieces and one piece of wadding for the tail; two white felt cheeks; two pink noses; two pink tongues; four white eye bases; four black eyes; four white felt paws; and twelve pink paw pads.

Step 2

Pair up all the pieces (excluding the body), with right sides together. Machine sew around the edge of each pair, make a slit in the centre on one side (with the exception of the tongue and tail) and turn through. For the tongue, leave the top straight edge

open and turn through from there. For the tail, place the wadding under the fabric and machine sew around the edge, leaving the base part (straight edge) of the tail open. Use a long tool to help you poke the tail through. (See page 55 for a more detailed explanation on machining and turning through.)

Step 3

Pin the pink nose onto the centre of the white cheeks and machine it all the

way round. Then machine sew the whisker details using black cotton.

Step 4

Machine sew the 'turned through' black eyes onto the 'turned through' white eye bases and then position the eyes onto the front body piece and sew in place. Next position the cheek piece with the top of the tongue inserted underneath and then machine sew this in place all the way round to secure.

Day Two

Step 5
Position the pink paw pads onto the white paws and machine sew in place.

Step 6
Position both paws onto the front piece of the cat body and machine sew all around to secure in place.

Step 7
Place the two cat body pieces right sides together and insert the wadded tail between the two layers at the base of the body where you want its final position to be. Machine sew all around the body except along the base. Repeat this machine line again for extra strength.

Step 8
With the cat still inside out, pin the base circle in place and machine sew it all around, leaving an opening to turn the cat through. Repeat this machine line again for extra strength.

Step 9
Fill the cat's body with the polystyrene balls and hand sew the opening securely. When pouring the polystyrene balls into the cat's body, ask someone to help you because the little balls have a tendency to jump everywhere.

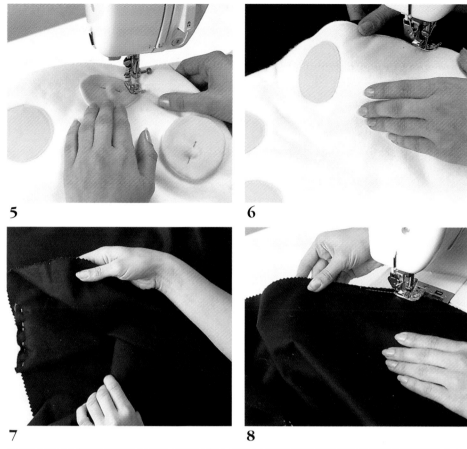

5

6

7

8

Machine sewing

A plain seam sewn with a straight stitch is the simplest and most versatile means of joining two pieces of fabric together. If you are not used to sewing with a machine, always pin your lengths of fabric together before sewing.

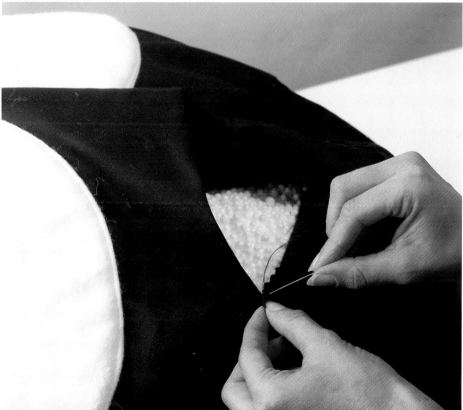

9

Sports peg rail and PVC kit bag

A handy peg rail will help children keep their sports kit together and easy to find. They will enjoy transporting it all in a specially designed PVC kit bag.

Sweaty sports kit left festering in a bag under the bed is not the most pleasant of treats to come across – especially when it has been there for some time! So what better way to encourage your children to hang up their kit than their very own themed peg rail and wipeable sports kit bag? At least then you will have a reasonable idea of where to find the offending items!

The peg rail is very easy to make and can be topped with any sort of ball, from tennis to rugby, and from hockey to netball – whichever is your child's favourite sport. I have used footballs here.

The sports bag is made from cotton-backed PVC, which means that it has the added benefit of being wipeable whenever necessary. Instead of putting your child's initials on the bag you could put their full name or nickname, date of birth or favourite team or player's name and number. Make sure you use a heavy-duty needle on your sewing machine when sewing the PVC. Try a practice run on any offcuts because you will find PVC slightly different to work on than other fabrics.

Planning your time

DAY ONE
AM: Prepare peg rail, prime and paint it

PM: Make clay footballs

DAY TWO
AM: Cut out the paper templates and bag pieces, glue on numbers and letters

PM: Machine sew bag components together

Tools and materials

For the peg rail:
A piece of MDF (medium density fibreboard) 2 cm (¾ in) thick, measuring 65 x 13 cm (26 x 5 in)

5 pieces of wooden dowelling 7 cm (3 in) long, 1 cm (⅜ in) in diameter

Drill

Primer paint

Gloss paint

Permanant marker pen

Wood glue

White modelling clay

For the sports bag:
Cotton backed PVC – one colour for the bag, and two colours for the trimmings

160 cm (64 in) of brightly coloured rope

All-purpose glue

Thick brown paper for template

1

2

3

Day One

Step 1

For the peg rail, mark off five evenly spaced points on the piece of MDF. Using the drill with a head piece the same size as the dowelling, drill five holes into the base, just stopping before you go all the way through the wood. Apply primer to the rail base and wooden dowel pieces and, when dry, paint them with the gloss paint, for a tough durable finish. When the paint is dry, place a little spot of wood glue into each hole along the rail base and insert the dowel pieces.

Step 2

Using the white modelling clay, roll out five disc shapes, each 1 cm (⅜ in) thick, and make an indentation into the back of each one the same size as the dowel pieces. Bake according to the manufacturer's instructions. When cool, use the permanent marker pen to draw on the football design (see template on page 72). You may want to do this in pencil first. Place a little spot of wood glue into the indentation on the back of each disc and glue onto the end of each piece of dowel on the peg rail base.

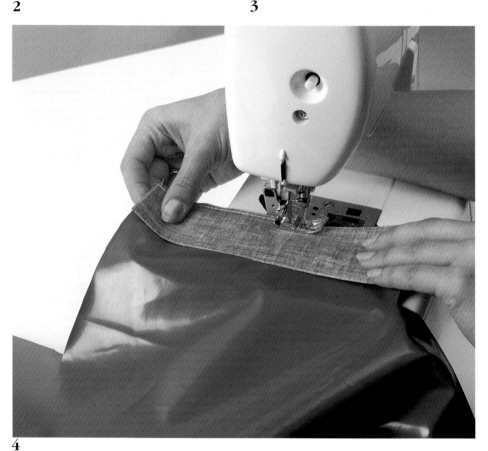

4

Day Two

Step 3

Following the pattern on page 72, cut out a template for the T-shirt bag from brown paper and then cut out the PVC. You will need two blue T-shirt base pieces excluding the red trim edges marked by dotted lines; four pieces of red sleeve borders, 5 x 20 cm (2 x 8 in); two pieces of red bottom trim 5 x 74 cm (2 x 30 in); one white circle 30 cm (12 in) in diameter, initials, number and full stops in whichever contrast colour you prefer.

Step 4

Place the red sleeve and base trims right sides facing down onto the dotted line edges of the blue T-shirt and machine sew on along the edge. Do this for both the front and back pieces of the T-shirt.

Step 5

Using the all-purpose glue, stick the number onto the white circle. When this has dried stick the circle onto the front piece of the T-shirt. Glue the initials and full stops under the circle.

Step 6

Place the right sides of the T-shirt together and machine sew down side A from top to bottom (see pattern on page 72).

Step 7

Open out the two sides flat with the wrong sides still facing you and fold over the top 5 cm (2 in) of side B all the way across the two T-shirt pieces and machine sew. This makes the rope channel.

Step 8

Fold the two sides back so that the T-shirt is right sides together again. Starting in a direct line from under the channel opening, machine sew along sides C and D.

Step 9

Turn the bag through the right way round and feed the rope into the channel. Take the rope ends and tie them together into a large knot.

Where to buy rope

I bought my rope from a boating shop. Ship's chandlers sell coloured ropes of varying thicknesses that are usually used for hoisting up sails!

5

6

7

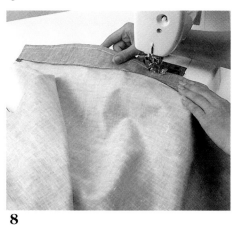

8

9

Fabric-fronted shelf units

These attractive storage units provide an opportunity for 'everything in its place'. They are easy to make and the decoration can be matched to any colour scheme.

Planning your time

DAY ONE
AM: Prime and paint shelf unit, trims and wooden dowelling

PM: Glue on edge trims; stick on Velcro

DAY TWO
AM: Make fabric cover panel

PM: Make clay fittings and screw in cup hooks

Tools and materials

Wooden shelf unit

Pre-cut MDF (medium density fibreboard) edge trims (see Suppliers on page 78)

Wood primer

Eggshell or gloss paint in two colours

Paintbrushes

Wood glue

Masking tape

Self-adhesive Velcro

Cotton-backed PVC fabric (width and height of shelf unit plus an extra 8 cm [3 in] all around)

Wooden dowelling, 1.5 cm (⅝ in) in diameter, and 6 cm (2½ in) wider than the unit

Coloured modelling clay

6 plastic cup hooks

Bradawl

Small tacks

Hammer

Teaching children to be organized and tidy needs a lot of patience – they sometimes think that wardrobes and drawers are for filling to excess and when it comes to retrieving a particular item can pull absolutely everything out until they find what they are after. It is possible, though, to make putting away and finding things less frustrating for them, by providing enough practical storage space. Open shelving is ideal because everything is immediately visible – but of course that does not guarantee that each shelf will be kept tidy!

For this project I took a plain, freestanding wooden shelf unit, painted it in a bright colour, then added some fun shelf trims to the edge of each shelf and made a PVC cotton-backed fabric panel for the front. The cover simply rolls up and down and is hooked into place with white plastic cup hooks.

This idea can be translated to any size of shelf unit and, if you wanted, you could add a fabric panel to both the sides. As these side panels would be kept permanently rolled down you would not need to put hooks into the sides.

Day One

Step 1
Apply primer to all the bare wood. Then, using the two different colour paints, paint the frame of the shelf unit in one colour and the shelves and edge trims in the other colour. Leave to dry.

Step 2
Apply wood glue to the front edge of each shelf and fix the edge trim in place. Use masking tape to secure it in place until the glue has completely dried.

Step 3
Take one side of the self-adhesive Velcro tape, cut it to the width of the top shelf and then stick it on.

Day Two

Step 4
Cut the cotton-backed PVC to just under the total width of the unit – this is so that some of the brightly painted verticals will show either side of the cover. Hem the top by turning it over 5 cm (2 in) and machine sewing it.

Step 5
Take the other side of the piece of Velcro, stick it over the top hem of the fabric panel and machine sew it in place for added strength.

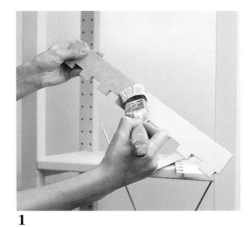

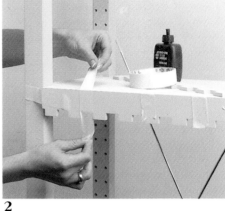

1

2

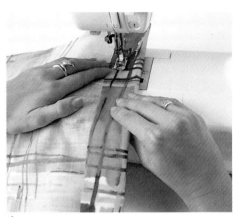

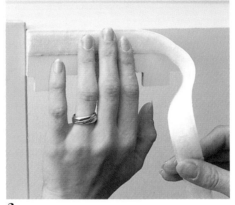

3

4

5

Painting the unit

Use an oil-based paint to paint the shelf unit as this will result in a more durable finish. Make sure that you paint the unit in the direction of its wood grain. Thus, apply paint in up and down strokes to the vertical struts, and paint the shelves from side to side.

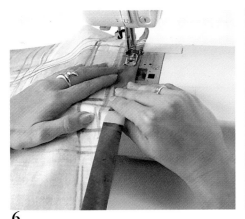

6

7

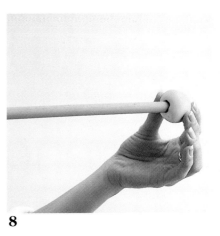

8

Step 6

Working on the bottom of the fabric panel, turn over 1 cm (⅜ in) and machine sew a hem. Then turn over a further 5 cm (2 in) and machine sew this on the edge so that it forms an open channel – this is where the wooden dowelling will be fed through. (PVC cotton does not fray, so you do not need to neaten the side edges.)

Step 7

Apply primer to the wooden dowelling and leave to dry. Then paint the wooden dowelling with your chosen colour, and, when it is dry, feed it into the bottom channel of the fabric panel. Make sure that it protrudes an equal amount on each side. Then, using small tacks, tack from the back of the panel to secure the dowelling in place – make sure the tack is hammered right through the fabric and into the dowelling.

Step 8

Using the modelling clay, roll a round ball for each end of the dowelling, one in each colour. Before baking the balls use the dowelling to make an indentation into each of them to ensure that they will fit neatly onto it. Bake the balls following the manufacturer's instructions. When they are cool, apply a small amount of wood glue onto the end of each piece of wooden dowelling, and then stick the clay ball in place.

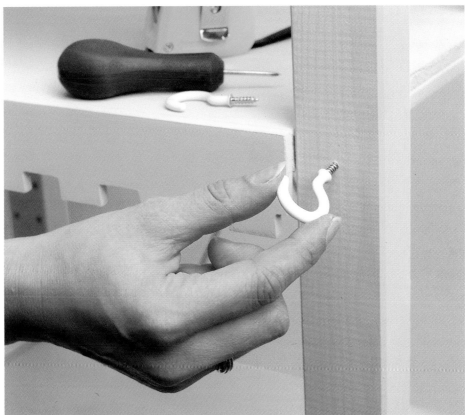

9

Step 9

Using a pencil, mark where the plastic hooks are going to be positioned. Ideally, the first pair should be a quarter of the way down the vertical struts, the second pair halfway down the struts and the third pair three quarters of the way down. Then use the bradawl to make the holes, and screw the hooks in place. Finally, stick the fabric panel up onto the Velcro strip at the top.

'Daisy Daisy' noticeboard

An easy-to-change noticeboard is ideal for children to display an endless array of drawings, photographs and messages, without spoiling the walls of their rooms.

Planning your time

DAY ONE
Prepare all your materials and staple the fabric to the board

DAY TWO
Attach ribbons and shapes

Tools and materials

A piece of MDF (medium density fibreboard) 90 x 60 cm (36 x 24 in)

115 g (4 oz) wadding, measuring 90 x 60 cm (36 x 24 in)

Fabric to fit the size of your board plus 8 cm (3 in) extra all round

1 cm (⅜ in) wide satin ribbon in two colours

Decorative-headed tacks

Felt in two colours

Pinking shears

Scissors

Staple gun

Hammer

Children love to colonize their rooms, but their belongings often end up all over the place. This is quite natural, but with careful thought and planning for their storage and shelving requirements you can help to encourage your children to be a little tidier.

This fun noticeboard is ideal for holding pictures, cards and any small items that are likely to be lost. You can make it as large or as small as you want and, of course, change the number of ribbons that criss-cross it so that more items can be held in place or displayed.

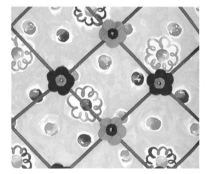

You can also choose your own theme for the fabric cut-out shapes that cover and secure where the ribbons cross and continue whatever theme is in the design of the fabric. Or you could cut out the letters in your child's name and use these to cover where the ribbons cross.

For a more durable finish I recommend that the piece of fabric that you use to cover the noticeboard is given an anti-stain treatment first. This means that any dirty finger marks can be easily washed off.

Day One

Step 1

Cut the wadding to the same size as the piece of MDF. Place the board on top of the fabric, allow 8 cm (3 in) all the way round and cut with pinking shears.

Step 2

Place the fabric wrong side up and then place the wadding on top and finally place the board on top of the wadding.

Step 3

Pull the fabric taut, and along the middle of each side place a few staples.

Step 4

Fold each corner over neatly and secure with staples, making sure that the fabric is pulled very tightly.

Day Two

Step 5

Turn the board over so that the right side is uppermost. Lay strips of ribbon in one colour from side to side diagonally across the board. Cut the strips, leaving an extra 8 cm (3 in) at each end.

Anti-stain treatment

Fabric can be given an anti-stain or waterproofing treatment, and it is possible to do this at home using DIY kits available from department stores. This treatment will give your noticeboard the added benefit of being wipeable.

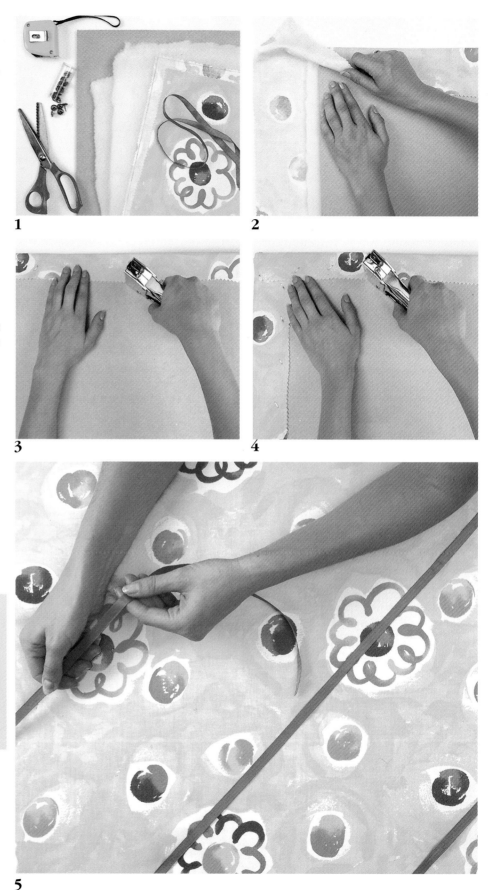

1

2

3

4

5

6

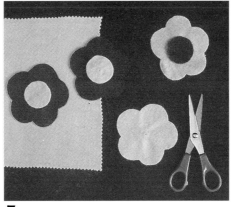

7

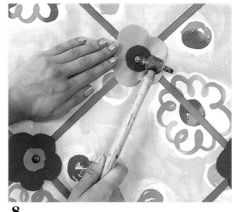

8

Step 6

Now lay strips of ribbon in the other colour in the opposite direction. Again cut the ribbon strips, leaving an extra 8 cm (3 in) at each end.

Step 7

Cut out the daisy shapes and centre piece from felt in alternating colours, following the template on page 70.

Step 8

Place a daisy and its centre over each point where the ribbons cross and secure in place with a decorative-headed tack.

Step 9

Turn the board over and secure all the ribbon ends in place using a staple gun, making sure to pull them very taut. Finally, fasten two picture hooks into the back of the board for hanging.

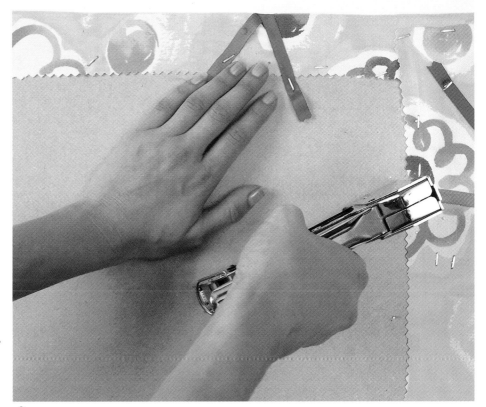

9

Tacking the fabric

If you do not have a staple gun you can use fine nail tacks and a hammer, but you may require assistance to help hold the fabric taut.

Noughts and crosses headboard game

This giant noughts and crosses headboard game is positioned so that your children can enjoy a last challenge or two before settling down for the night.

Planning your time

DAY ONE
AM: Cut out all the pieces

PM: Make up the board

DAY TWO
AM: Make up the playing pieces, paint the dowelling

PM: Make the clay shapes

Tools and materials

Felt in four different colours for the board, dividing lines and playing pieces

55 g (2 oz) wadding for the playing pieces

115 g (4 oz) wadding for the board

A piece of wooden dowelling 92 cm (37 in) long

Wood glue

Primer paint

Eggshell or gloss paint

Two colours of modelling clay to match the playing pieces

Heavy brown paper

Scissors

Self-adhesive Velcro pads

Getting children to bed is not the easiest of tasks, especially when they have friends to 'sleep over' and it is practically impossible to get them to settle down. That is why the logic behind this headboard game is ideal, because they can play with it while in bed.

The 'board' is made from felt and the playing pieces simply attach to it with Velcro. The whole game then hangs from the loops on a piece of wooden dowelling supported by two wall hooks.

This project can be adapted to make other board games. If you like a challenge you could try chess, draughts or snakes and ladders. For a large-scale game, however, it might be more practical to make a board that could be used on the floor. These games are ideal to take when travelling, because they can be folded up and packed in a bag.

Day One

Step 1

Cut out three pieces of blue felt for the hanging loops, each measuring 40 x 18 cm (16 x 7 in); two felt pieces and one piece of wadding for the board, each measuring 90 x 90 cm (36 x 36 in); and four white felt pieces for the dividing lines, each measuring 90 x 5 cm (36 x 2 in).

Step 2

Mark out onto one piece of the blue felt board where the white lines should be positioned so that they divide the board evenly into nine squares. Machine sew them in place along each long side.

Step 3

Fold the felt loops in half lengthways, right sides together. Machine sew along the long side and then turn it through to the right way round. You do not need to sew the two ends. Position the three loops pointing downwards at the top edge of the board on the right side and machine the ends right onto the edge.

Step 4

Place the two blue board pieces right sides together and then place the wadding underneath them. Machine sew all the way round, leaving about 20 cm (8 in) open along the bottom. Pull the board through the opening and then hand sew it to close.

1

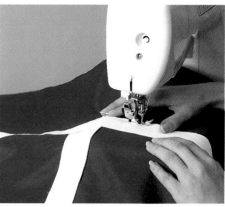

2

3

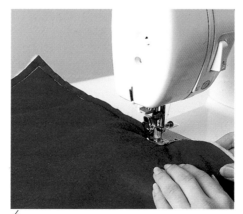

4

Choosing felt

Felt comes in different qualities and it is worth buying a good weight felt for the game board, but use a lighter weight one for the playing pieces.

Day Two

Step 5

Trace the outlines on page 70 and enlarge to make templates for the noughts and crosses out of brown paper, remembering to allow a little extra all the way around for the seam allowance. Cut out five pairs of each shape and a piece of wadding for each pair.

Step 6

Place each pair of noughts and crosses right sides together, and place the wadding underneath. For each cross, machine sew all the way around, leaving a small opening. Pull the cross through this opening and then hand sew it to close. For each nought, machine sew all the way around, then make a slit on the back through one layer of fabric and pull the nought through the slit to turn it the right way round.

Step 7

Attach two pieces of self-adhesive Velcro to the back of each nought and cross, and then sew up the slit on the back of each nought.

Step 8

Paint the piece of dowelling with primer and leave to dry. Then paint with a satin-finish or gloss-finish paint and leave to dry.

Step 9

Make a nought and cross shape out of modelling clay. For the cross, roll out two long sausage shapes, then cut one in half and stick the two halves onto the other piece. For the nought, roll out a ball, then gently roll it flat and make an indentation into it. Bake the shapes following the manufacturer's instructions. Stick them onto the wooden dowelling using a touch of wood glue. Feed this through the felt loops and the board is ready for hanging.

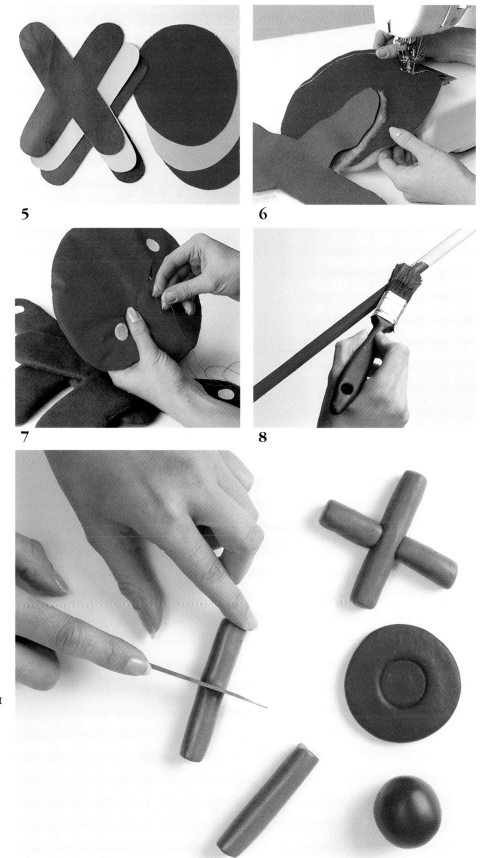

5

6

7

8

9

Eight-drawer chest

A little time and planning, and multicoloured splashes of paint, transform an ordinary chest of drawers into an exciting and unusual piece of furniture.

I have always been a firm believer that it is not worth spending a fortune on children's furniture, because not only does it receive poor treatment but all too quickly the children grow out of it. Fortunately, the shops nowadays are full of self-assembly and plain wooden furniture that is ideal for applying a fancy finish to.

The plain eight-drawer chest which I used for this project started off its life as a very basic unit, but with the addition of some fun colour, tissue papers and unusual handles it has assumed a new identity. For simplicity you could just pick out two colours to paint the drawers in and create a quite dramatic chequerboard effect – especially if painted in black and white.

Look out for really eye-catching handles or buy plain wooden ones and paint them to match the unit. You could also make interesting shapes out of modelling clay and glue them onto the fronts of the wooden handles. Feet added to the unit give it elegance and, painted appropriately, it would even be worthy of being kept in an adult's room.

Planning your time

DAY ONE
AM: Sand, drill and colourwash the unit and drawers

PM: Colourwash the feet and glue them on, cut and attach paper shapes

DAY TWO
AM: Varnish the unit and drawers twice

PM: Varnish the unit a third time and attach the handles

Tools and materials

One plain eight-drawer chest

Sandpaper

Drill

Different coloured water-based paints

Paintbrushes

Plastic cups

4 wooden door handles – for the feet

Wood glue

Different coloured thick tissue paper

Scissors

Artist's spray glue

Clear matt varnish

8 interesting handles

Screwdriver

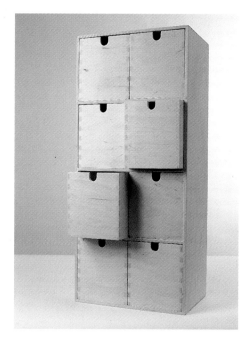

1

Day One

Step 1

Take each drawer out of the unit. The backs of the drawers will become the fronts as the existing fronts have finger holes in them.

Step 2

Mark a cross in the centre of the back of each drawer and drill a hole to fit the screw size of the drawer handles.

Step 3

Then gently sand down the whole of the unit and the drawers, making sure you work in the direction of the grain of the wood. Wipe each piece with a slightly damp cloth to remove any wood dust.

2

3

Step 4

Take the paint in the colour that you want to paint the body of the unit and pour a little of it into a plastic cup. Now add water to dilute the paint down – approximately eight parts of water to one part of paint. As the unit will be colourwashed it is not necessary to prime it first. Apply the diluted paint using light, fluid movements and painting in the direction of the wood grain (see *Colourwashing* below).

Step 5

Dilute all the other paints that you are going to use – eight parts of water to one part of paint – and then colourwash all the drawers.

Step 6

Colourwash the four wooden handles for the feet in the same colours as the drawer fronts.

4

5

6

Colourwashing

Colourwashing is one of the simplest and most effective ways of painting wood. It picks up and highlights the grain of the wood beautifully, and thus it is not necessary to prime the wood first. As the paint is watered down it is vital that you start off with a water-based emulsion – the finished effect is slightly translucent.

Apply the watered-down paint mixture with light strokes of the paintbrush, working in the same direction as the grain of the wood. You will need to work quite quickly because this solution will be absorbed into the wood. As only small quantities of paint are used, it is more economical to buy little tester pots.

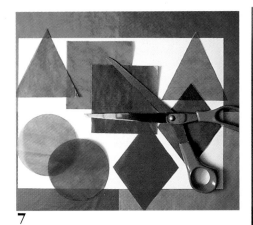

7

Step 7

Cut out two each of circles, squares, triangles and diamonds from the coloured paper to a size that will fit comfortably on the front of each drawer.

Step 8

Using the spray glue, lightly spray each paper shape and then paste one shape onto the front of each drawer.

Step 9

Use wood glue to attach the wooden feet to the bottom of the unit. When they have just begun to set, varnish the bottom of the unit and leave it overnight to dry.

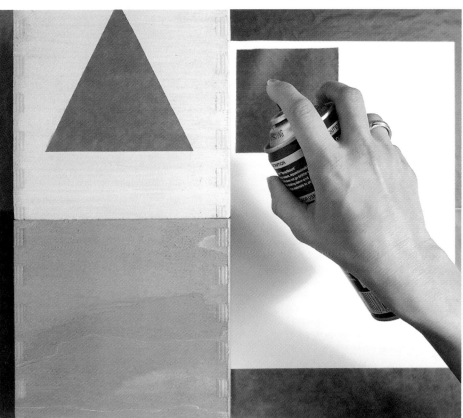

8

9

Day Two

Step 10

Varnish the whole unit and drawers with clear matt varnish. Ideally you should apply three to four coats, letting each one dry in between for approximately 4 hours.

Step 11

When the varnish is completely dry, screw on the handles to each drawer front.

Varnishing

Varnishing an item of furniture helps to protect it against wear and tear. It also gives you the option of changing the surface from an eggshell finish to matt to gloss. Durable, hard varnishes are slightly yellow in colour, while colourless varnishes offer less protection.

I recommend that you select a matt finish to your varnish, as it does not catch the light and show up all the irregularities on the furniture.

10

11

Playing card curtains and tie-backs

Make bedtime more fun for children with these playing card shapes. I have chosen bright primary blue to go with red instead of the traditional black.

Planning your time

DAY ONE
AM: Cut out the shapes

PM: Make up all the padded shapes

DAY TWO
AM: Cut out tabs and attach to the curtains and sew on shapes

PM: Make the tie-backs

Tools and materials

Fabric for the tab tops, shapes and tie-backs

55 g (2 oz) wadding

Fabric for the curtains and lining (twice the width of the window)

Scissors

Thick brown paper for cutting templates

The approach to 'dressing' windows has changed dramatically since the 1980s. Now there are many more options to choose from than just a plain curtain rail. Curtain poles are extremely popular and look particularly good in children's bedrooms. Avoid the sophisticated wrought-iron poles and instead opt for chunky wooden ones that are more adaptable to decoration. If you buy them in their natural wood state they are very easy to paint in a bright colour.

The tab-topped heading on these curtains is also easy to make, though the padded shapes may take a little time to master. Once you have perfected making these shapes, however, you will have no difficulty with any of the other projects in the book that use a similar technique.

Tab-topped curtains save on curtain tape and hooks as the tabs are simply fed onto the wooden pole. This type of heading does make it a little difficult for the curtains to be pulled back as far as you may wish, however, so I have designed matching tie-backs to hold back the bulk of the curtains during the day.

Day One

Step 1

Trace around the playing card templates on page 73 onto brown paper and cut them out. Enlarge two of them for the tie-backs.

Step 2

Measure the width of the curtain and work out how many tabs and shapes you will need. I have placed mine 15 cm (6 in) apart. Then, using your templates, cut out as many pairs of shapes as you need. Also cut one piece of wadding for each shape.

Step 3

Place right sides together of each pair of shapes and then place on top of the wadding. Machine all the way round the shape. Make a cut in the middle of each shape through one of the pieces of fabric and pull the whole shape through. Repeat this for all the shapes, including the two large ones.

Day Two

Step 4

Cut out the required number of tabs, each measuring 40 x 20 cm (16 x 8 in). Fold the tabs in half lengthways, with right sides together, and machine sew around the two sides leaving a short top edge open. Turn through the top edge and press with an iron.

Step 5

Separately hem your curtain fabric and lining (at the bottom), but do not machine them together. Lay the curtain and lining right sides together, then fold the tabs in half and pin them on along the top edge, leaving 15 cm (6 in) between each. The folded length of the tabs should be between the two pieces of fabric. Now machine a straight line all the way across the top edge of the curtain to secure the tabs in place.

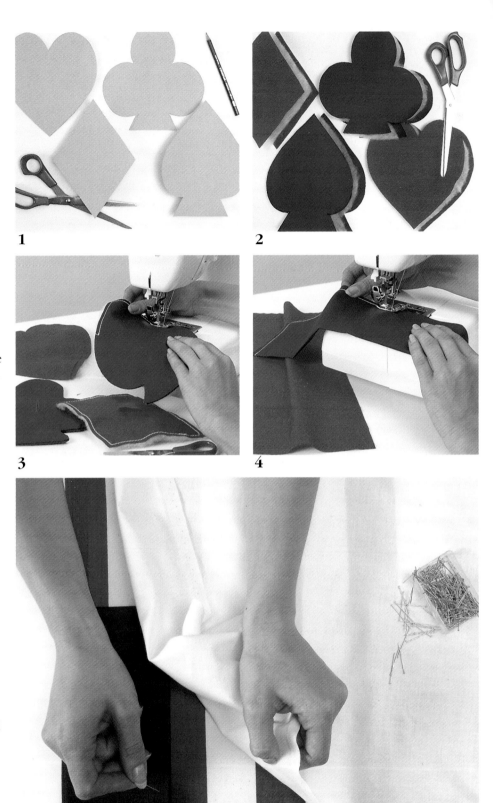

1

2

3

4

5

6

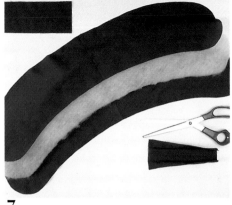

7

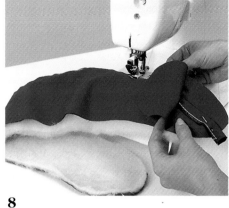

8

Step 6

Still with the right side of the curtains together, machine sew down the side edges of the curtains to secure lining and curtain fabric together. Then turn the curtains the right way round and hand sew a shape onto each tab.

Step 7

Cut out the tie-back pieces. These are crescent shapes 70 x 15 cm (28 x 6 in) with rounded ends. For each tie-back you will need two pieces of crescent-shaped fabric and one piece of wadding. You will also need two tabs 18 x 8 cm (7 x 3 in), one for each end. Take the tabs and fold both long edges into the centre, fold together again into the centre and press with an iron. Then machine sew a line down the centres to secure them in their folded-up state.

Step 8

Take the crescent-shaped pairs and sandwich them right sides together with the wadding underneath. Insert the tabs, one at each end, folded in half lengthways between the fabric, and machine all the way round, securing the tabs in place. Leave a small opening along one side and turn the tie-back through the opening and hand sew it to close.

Step 9

Take the extra-large wadded shapes and hand sew them onto one end of the tie-back – not the middle!

9

Machine sewing and turning through

Many of the projects in the book include making shaped fabric pieces that need to be machine sewn on the wrong sides and turned through to the right side. Corners need to be clipped – to do this cut across the seam allowance after sewing the seam, but leave at least 6 mm (¼ in) between the seam and the cut edge of the fabric. Likewise on fabric shapes make little snips into the seam allowance, but be careful not to get too close to the seam. This will prevent pulling once it is turned through.

Elephant pocket storage system

This reliable elephant carries lots of jewel-bright pockets of different shapes and sizes to help your children keep track of personal accessories and special treasures.

Children always seem to fill their pockets with the oddest assortment of what they regard as basic essentials. So I have taken this theme and turned it into a larger and more practical version. A friendly elephant forms the base upon which hangs an assortment of bright pockets decorated with a variety of colourful trinkets.

I have used wadding in making the elephant base to give it more substance, and it also helps to accentuate the feet, ear and eye machine-sewn detailing.

Make sure you choose a heavyweight fabric for the pocket system base as it will need to bear the strain of a great number of items jammed into the pockets. You can make as many pockets as you like, large and small, and, of course, they do not have to form part of an animal. You could machine sew them onto a plain piece of fabric. Sew a channel across it top and bottom, and place pieces of wooden dowelling into the channels to help the pocket system to hang better.

Planning your time

DAY ONE
AM: Cut out all the pieces and machine the pockets together

PM: Machine sew body together and attach pockets

DAY TWO
AM: Embroider facial and foot details and sew on decorations

Tools and materials

Heavyweight fabric for the pocket system base

Brightly coloured fabrics for the pockets, preferably cotton drill

115 g (4 oz) wadding for the elephant's body

Decorations, beads and foil shapes, or fabric pens

Scissors

Chalk

Day One

Step 1

Using the chalk, draw the elephant shape onto the fabric, following the templates on page 74. Cut out two elephant shapes in fabric, and cut one in wadding.

Step 2

Following the shape of the elephant's back, cut out two purple 'rugs' from the cotton drill – the pockets will later be attached to this rug.

Step 3

Using different coloured cotton drill fabrics, cut out four different shaped pockets that will neatly fit onto the purple 'rug' – you will need two of each pocket shape.

Step 4

Place the right sides of the purple rug together and machine sew around the three edges, leaving the top curved edge open. Turn it through to the right side and press with a warm iron.

Step 5

Place each pair of pockets right sides together. Sew round all the edges leaving a small opening on one side. Turn them all through to the right side and press with a warm iron. Then hand sew the opening (see page 25).

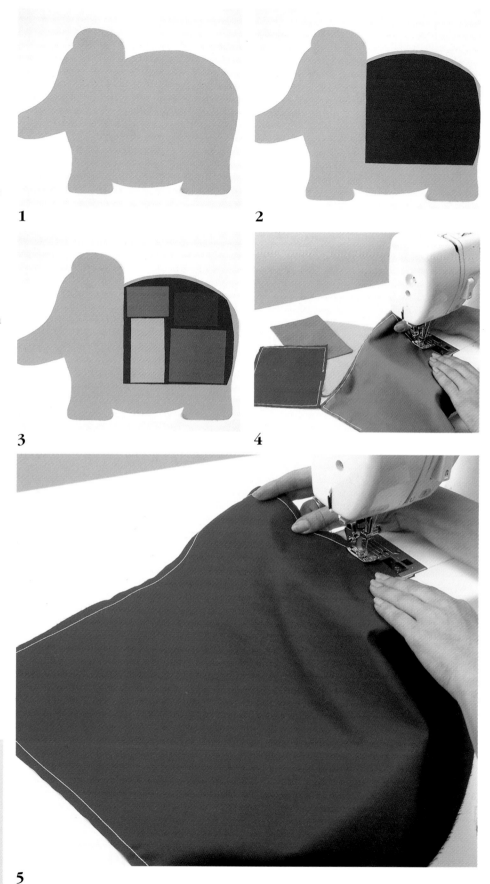

1

2

3

4

5

Planning the pockets

Bear in mind the height of your children when making the pocket system. They must be able to reach into the pockets with ease. In general the younger the child, the larger, wider and shallower the pockets should be.

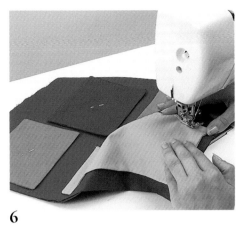

6

7

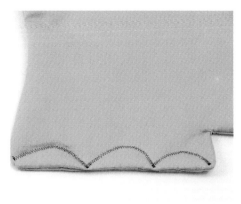

8

Step 6

Pin the pockets in position on the purple rug and machine sew around three sides of each pocket, leaving the top edge open. Repeat this machine line for extra strength.

Step 7

Place the elephant body pieces right sides together, but sandwich the now completed purple rug in between them with the curved tops lined up. Place the wadding at the back of this 'sandwich' and machine sew all the way around the elephant, leaving the side seam open at the rear of the elephant. Repeat this machine line for extra strength. Pull the whole elephant through the open seam to turn the right way round and then hand sew the rear seam.

Day Two

Step 8

Using a zig-zag stitch, machine sew the feet, ear and eye details with a contrasting colour thread.

Step 9

Sew the decorations onto the front of the pockets and over the eye. Sew two fabric loops onto the back of the elephant so that it can be attached to the wall. Finally, sew a curly shoelace onto the elephant for a tail.

9

Decorating the pockets

Besides sewing on beads and foils you could also decorate the pockets with fabric pens. They come in a variety of bright colours and textures. Also look out for glitter pens that dispense glitter in a glue solution.

Porthole blackboard

Small children may chalk away to their hearts' content on this blackboard in the shape of a porthole. The fishy dusters and pockets continue the seaside theme.

Normally parents try to keep their children's artistic endeavours off the walls, but here I have created a 'chalk board' wall, which children can happily attack with as many colours of chalk as they wish. Blackboard paint is available in 1 litre cans and is applied straight onto a plain painted wall. There is nothing to stop you from painting a whole wall with this paint and the beauty of it is that you can paint over it with ordinary paint at any time. A thick cloth is all it takes to remove any budding Picasso's works of art.

The cloth and chalks are all neatly kept together on a little hanging rail. Blue towelling pockets are perfect for keeping the chalk in and are decorated with a bright orange fish. The towelling starfish duster hangs from a plastic cup hook and can easily be washed out when it becomes too chalky. The theme for this project was the seashore, hence the fun porthole-shaped chalkboard, starfish and fish accessories, but you could change the shapes to suit your own children's favourite themes.

Planning your time

DAY ONE
AM: Cut template, spray frame and paint blackboard

PM: Make clay 'rivets' and starfish, screw hooks into wall

DAY TWO
AM: Make towelling pockets and orange fish

PM: Make the starfish duster and assemble the rail

Tools and materials

Thick brown paper for porthole template

Silver spray paint

Blackboard paint (see Suppliers on page 78)

Paintbrush

Yellow modelling clay

3 plastic cup hooks, wall plugs and drill

1.5 cm (⅝ in) wooden dowelling cut to the width of the porthole – 92 cm (37 in)

Orange oil-based paint

All-purpose glue

Blue and yellow towelling fabric

Orange cotton-drill fabric

55 g (2 oz) wadding for the fish shapes

60 cm (24 in) of orange satin ribbon, 1 cm (⅜ in) wide

12 cm (5 in) of blue satin ribbon, 1 cm (⅜ in) wide

Black fabric marker pen

Scissors

Artist's spray glue

Day One

Step 1

Draw out the design for the frame of the porthole onto brown paper (see page 75). Here the porthole frame is 9 cm (3½ in) deep around a centre circle of 72 cm (29 in) in diameter. Remember to leave some brown paper all the way around the outer edge of the porthole frame. After cutting out the frame apply some spray glue to the reverse sides of the template and then position it onto the wall at the desired height. Place the central cut-out circle in the middle. Make sure that all the edges are firmly stuck to the wall, then give the frame a light application of silver spray paint. Remove the templates from the wall.

Step 2

Carefully paint in the centre of the porthole with the blackboard paint, paying particular attention to the edges.

Step 3

Roll and cut out eight 4 cm (1½ in) circles, each 1.5 cm (⅝ in) thick out of the modelling clay. Using a sharp implement, score each with a 'rivet' down the centre. Bake following the manufacturer's instructions. When they are cool, place them on a piece of newspaper and lightly spray paint them silver. Mark off around the porthole eight evenly spaced crosses, and stick the silver rivets onto them using the all-purpose glue. Mark off under the porthole the positions for the three plastic hooks, drill the holes, insert a wall plug into each one and then screw in the cup hooks.

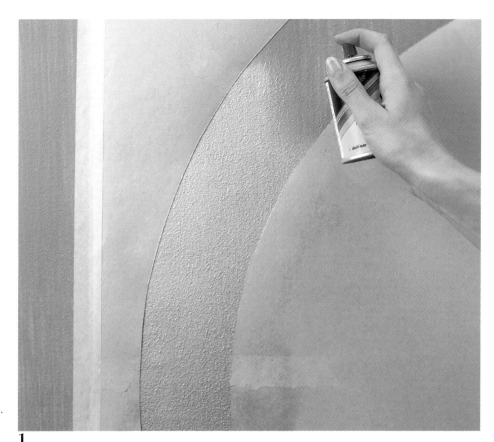

1

2

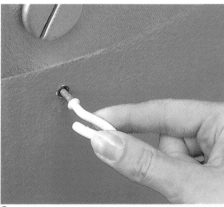

3

Drawing a circle

In order to draw a very large circle onto your template, use a drawing pin to attach a piece of string to the paper. Measure out the radius of your required circle and cut the string to this length, leaving enough to tie a pencil on the end. Then, holding your finger over the drawing pin, take the pencil and rotate it all the way round and draw the circle. Repeat this process, shortening the string by 9 cm (3½ in), to draw the inner edge of the porthole frame.

Step 4

Apply primer to thc wooden dowelling and leave to dry. Then paint the wooden dowelling with the orange paint and leave to dry. Using the yellow modelling clay, make two flat starfish shapes. Bake them following the manufacturer's instructions and, when cool, glue them to each end of the wooden dowelling.

Day Two

Step 5

Cut out the blue towelling pockets with the selvedge edge running across the top of them. You will need four pieces, each measuring 22 cm (9 in) wide and 25 cm (10 in) deep. Place them in pairs, right sides together, and machine sew the three sides. Then turn them the right way round.

Step 6

Cut the orange ribbon into four lengths of 15 cm (6 in) and hand sew two ribbon loops onto the back piece of each pocket.

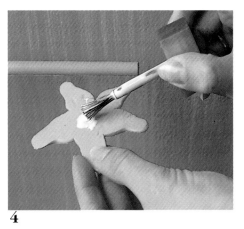

4

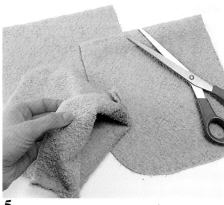

5

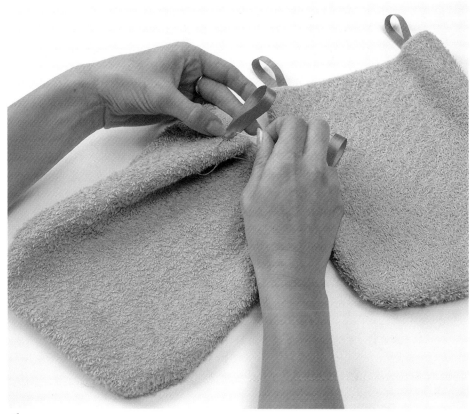

6

Using sprays

When using spray paint and spray glue make sure that the room you are working in is well ventilated. Shield off any surfaces near to the area that you are spraying – spray paint, especially, has a tendency to go everywhere.

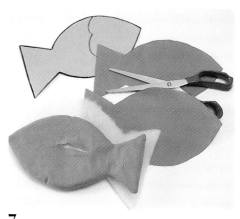

7

Step 7

Using the outlines on page 75, make a template for the fish out of brown paper. Use it to cut out four fish shapes from the orange fabric and two from the wadding. Place the fish in pairs, right sides together, and put the wadding at the back of the fabric. Machine sew all the way round. Then make a small slit through the centre of one piece of the orange fabric and turn the fish through to the right way round. Press with a warm iron.

Step 8

Use a black fabric marker pen to draw eyes and gills onto the fabric fish and then hand sew them onto the fronts of the blue pockets.

Step 9

Cut out a template for the starfish and use it to cut out two starfish shapes from the yellow towelling fabric. Place them right sides together and machine sew the starfish all the way around, leaving an opening on one leg. Turn it through the opening to the right way round and then hand sew to close. Hand sew the blue ribbon onto the end of a leg to form a loop.

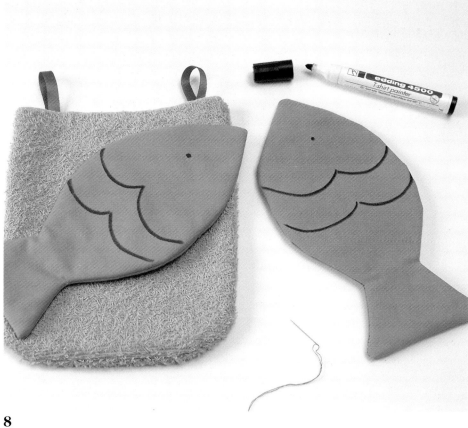

8

9

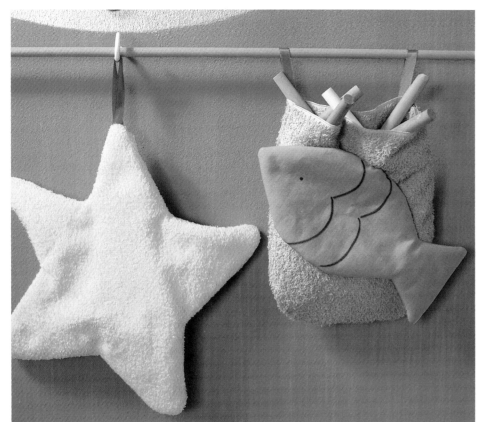

10

Step 10
Feed both the pockets onto the
dowelling through their loops and
position in place on the hooks. Attach
the starfish; simply hang it on the
middle hook by its loop.

Step 11
To complete the seaside theme I added
some pre-cut MDF trim to the skirting
board. Cut into a wave shape and
painted, it blends in with the skirting
while still providing a fun element to
the whole room scheme.

Using MDF trim

Pre-cut MDF trim is an easy way of adding
instant interest to straight edges. Painted
to blend in with or to contrast against
whatever you put it with, it provides a
finishing touch that helps to complete the
decoration of a room. (For stockist details
see Suppliers on page 78.)

11

Painted and stamped toy chest

Toy chests provide useful storage for a host of toys and games. This one sits on elegant feet in contrast to the friendly informality of its contents.

Planning your time

DAY ONE
AM: Drill, sand and prime chest

PM: Paint the chest

DAY TWO
AM: Assemble chest, apply stamp design and wavy line, and varnish

PM: Varnish two more times and tie on rope

Tools and materials

1 flat-packed self-assembly toy chest

Screwdriver

Drill and large drill bit

Masking tape

Fine-grade sandpaper

All-in-one white primer and undercoat

Selection of complementary emulsion paints

Paintbrushes, including a small artist's brush

Clear matt varnish

1.5 m (60 in) each of two colours of rope

Stamp design

Mini-roller

Dish for paint

A chest or blanket box is an invaluable item of furniture in a child's bedroom because it is perfect for storing big, bulky toys and games, while also doubling as a low table or a seat. Wooden chests come in all sorts of sizes. Some are plain, while others, like the one I transformed in this project, have a little detailing cut into the front panel and, more importantly, have feet. I always feel that a piece of furniture with feet on it immediately takes on a smarter look – raising this chest off the ground helps to give definition to its shape.

This toy chest came flat packed for self-assembly and I painted it with four bright pastel colours, then used a rubber stamp to apply the yellow block design and hand painted some wavy lines. The finishing touch was the addition of two chunky rope handles.

Since I wanted the box to have a chalky look to it I used water-based emulsion paints. But to make sure that it would survive any child's rough handling it was given a couple of coats of matt varnish. If you prefer, however, you could paint it with more durable gloss paint, although bear in mind that you will end up with a shiny effect.

1

2

3

Day One

Step 1

Using masking tape, mark off where the four holes for the rope handles will be on the lid of the chest. I positioned them 15 cm (6 in) from the edge, with 20 cm (8 in) between the two holes of each handle. Use a large drill bit and drill the four holes through the lid.

Step 2

Gently sand all the surfaces of the chest on both sides to provide a 'key' for the primer. Wipe down with a damp cloth to remove all the wood dust.

Step 3

Apply a coat of an all-in-one quick primer and undercoat, and then leave to dry.

Step 4

Decide which sides of the chest to paint in which colour and then paint them using emulsion paint. Paint the pieces on both sides, leaving to dry. Also paint the feet.

4

Buying a toy chest

If you are going to buy a new toy or blanket chest to transform, look out for ones that are untreated – that is, not painted or varnished. This will save you time, as layers of paint and varnish must be removed before you can apply the decoration described here.

Day Two

Step 5

Assemble the chest following the manufacturer's instructions.

Step 6

Mark lightly with a pencil where you want to apply the stamp design. I placed designs over each of the drilled holes on the lid, two on the front and back and one on each side. Pour a little paint of the colour chosen for the design into a small dish, then roll the mini-roller onto the paint so that it is evenly covered. Roll the paint onto the stamp and gently apply the stamp to the chest.

Step 7

Using a pencil, lightly draw the wavy lines onto each side of the toy chest. When you are happy with them use the fine paintbrush to paint over the lines. As an extra touch I painted dots along the wavy line in a contrasting colour. Leave to dry.

Step 8

Using a clear matt varnish apply two to three coats all over the chest inside and out, making sure that each coat dries thoroughly in between.

Step 9

Thread the coloured rope through the holes and tie large, chunky knots on the underside of the lid. Remember to leave enough slack rope to form sufficient handles on the top of the chest.

Paints for stamping

You can buy special paints for stamping but I found that using a water-based emulsion paint worked just as well on the toy chest.

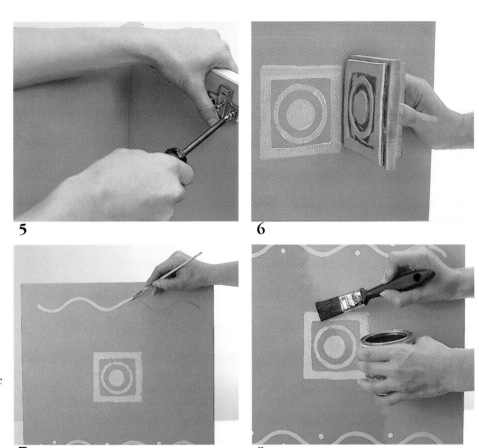

5

6

7

8

9

Templates

Bow bed canopy

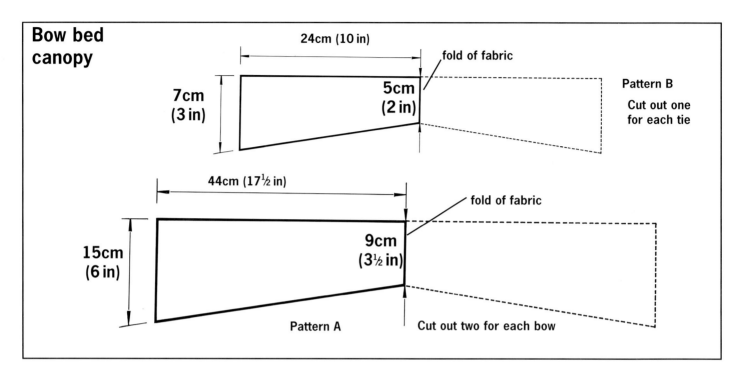

24cm (10 in)

7cm (3 in)

5cm (2 in)

fold of fabric

Pattern B

Cut out one for each tie

44cm (17½ in)

15cm (6 in)

9cm (3½ in)

fold of fabric

Pattern A

Cut out two for each bow

'Daisy Daisy' noticeboard

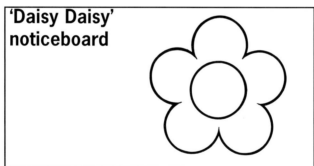

Noughts and crosses headboard game

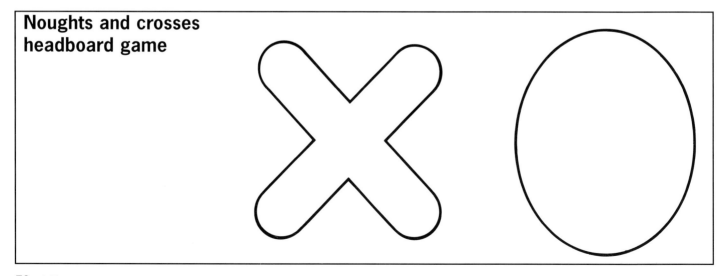

Templates

'Fat cat' bean bag

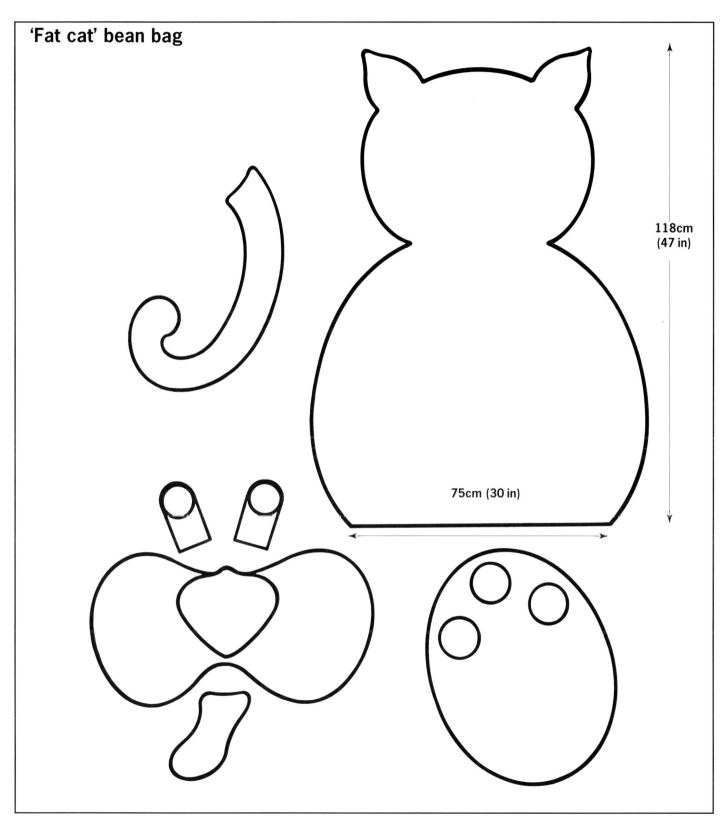

118cm
(47 in)

75cm (30 in)

Templates

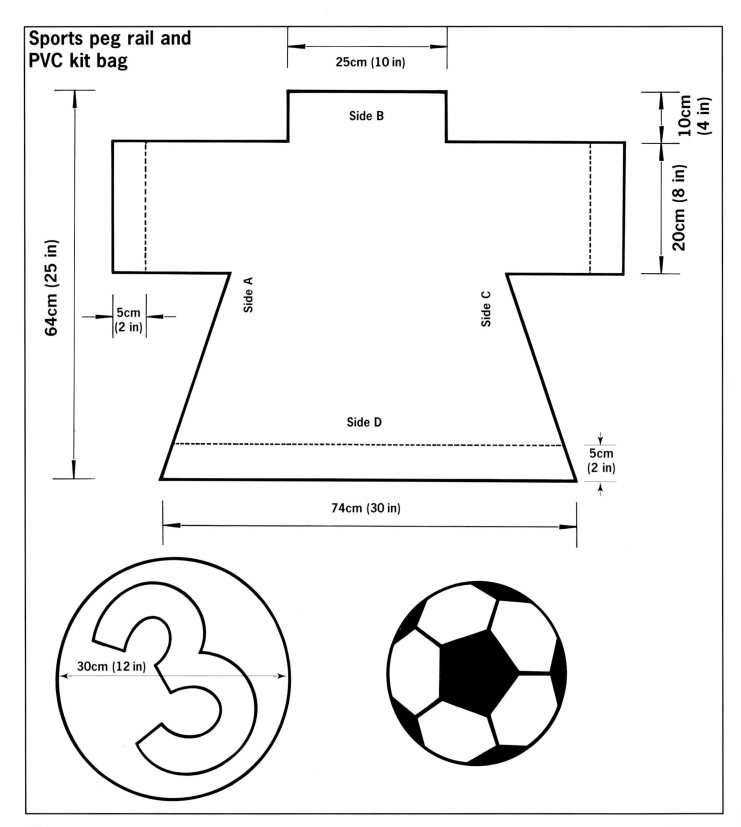

Sports peg rail and
PVC kit bag

25cm (10 in)

Side B

10cm (4 in)

20cm (8 in)

64cm (25 in)

5cm (2 in)

Side A

Side C

Side D

5cm (2 in)

74cm (30 in)

30cm (12 in)

Templates

Playing card curtains and tie-backs

Templates

Elephant pocket storage system

Templates

Porthole blackboard

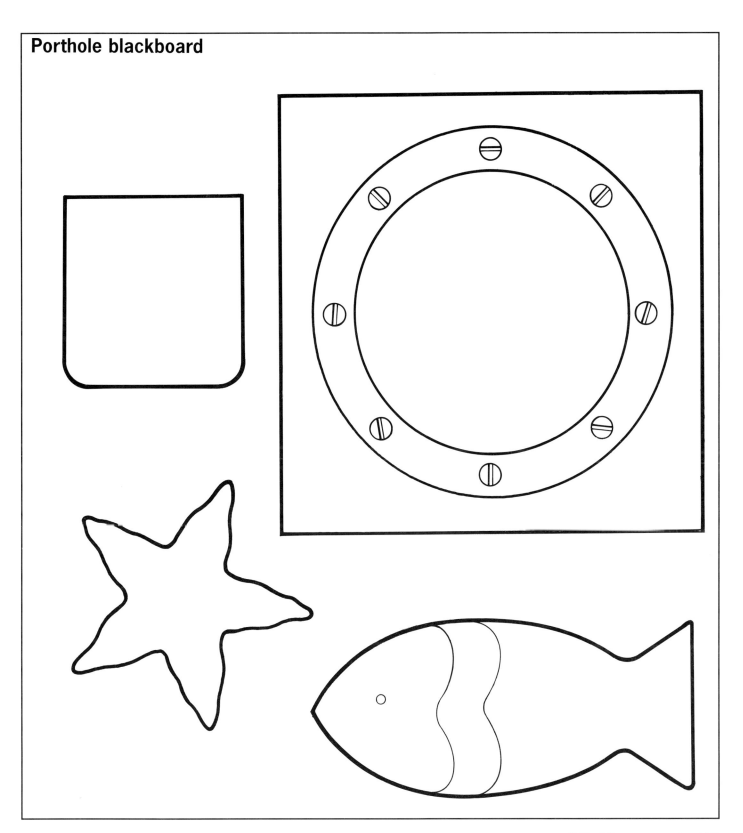

Glossary

MDF

Paint rollers

Masking tape

Drill bits

Anti-stain treatment
A finish that can be applied to fabric that gives it a stain-resistant surface.

Bradawl
A pointed tool used for marking the position for drilling a hole.

Colourwashing
A paint technique using watered-down emulsion paint to produce a subtle, chalky finish.

Dowelling
A length of round wood with a small diameter that can easily be cut to whatever length required.

Drill/drill bits
When buying a power drill make sure that the motor is powerful enough for all tasks; some drills with very low speed settings can be used for putting in screws. Bits are available in different sizes for drilling different-sized holes.

Filler
Ideal for filling holes, you can buy this in sachets and then add to water to make a paste or buy ready to use in a tub.

Fixing brackets for pelmet
These are attached to the wall and the pelmet is then attached to them.

French seam
A strong self-neatening seam that does not show any additional stitching line from the right side of the fabric. It can only be used on straight edges.

Glaze
Not to be confused with varnish. A glaze is a transparent medium to which colour is then added in the form of universal stainers (tinting colours).

Glue (all-purpose)
Can be used to stick a variety of materials together.

Glue (artist's spray glue)
Provides a light coating of glue out of a spray can.

Glue (wood)
Specifically for sticking items to wood.

Heavy brown paper
You can use brown paper, tracing paper or graph paper for making up a pattern or template.

Key
A rough surface suitable for the adhesion of paint or glue. A surface is usually keyed by rubbing with sandpaper.

Masking tape
Adhesive tape that has multiple uses and is ideal for masking off areas when painting. Available in different widths.

Medium density fibreboard (MDF)
Strong board made from soft wood fibres bonded together under pressure. It is sanded to produce an extremely smooth surface.

Modelling clay
Available in a variety of fun colours, to produce a hard, durable finish, it must be baked following the manufacturer's instructions .

Paint (emulsion)
A water-based paint that is easy to use and can be applied with a paintbrush or roller. It provides a water-resistant coating and is available in both matt and silk finishes. It is fast drying, so you need to work quickly with it.

Paint (oil-based)
This paint is available in gloss, eggshell and flat finishes and produces a durable and waterproof coating. It should be applied in layers, beginning with a primer and undercoat. Oil-based paints take longer to dry; large items should be left overnight to dry completely.

Paint rollers
These are ideal when you are painting large surface areas. Look out for patterned foam rollers that create an interesting texture on a flat surface.

Paintbrushes
Select an appropriate size brush according to the size of the item you are painting. Artists' brushes are useful for painting intricate details.

Priming
New or stripped wood should always be given a coat of primer paint before anything else is applied to it. This provides a good base for the top coat. Look out for primers and undercoats that are combined (all-in-one) as they will save valuable time. Previously painted wood does not need a primer, but sand down old paint to provide a good key for the undercoat.

Sanding block
Sandpaper wrapped around a wood block.

Selvedge
The edges of fabric that run down both sides of a length of fabric. These edges are finished off and do not fray.

Slipstitch
Used where a seam is required along the right side of a fabric.

Stamping
Making and applying inked designs to a smooth surface.

Staple gun
Larger than a domestic stapler, a staple gun is very powerful and can be used to secure fabric onto wood.

Tacks
Small, thin nails.

Varnish (oil-based)
This is the most traditional varnish, but is also the slowest drying, as it takes 12–24 hours.

Varnish (polyurethane)
This is available in matt, semi-gloss and gloss finishes. It dries within 4 hours and gives a very hardwearing surface.

Varnishing
Used for sealing a wooden surface and making it more durable. Most painted surfaces look better and last longer when treated to some coats of varnish, which provide a hardwearing finish.

Velcro
The brand name for a 'touch and close' fastener that consists of two pieces of nylon, one with tiny hooks and the other with small loops, which adhere when pressed together.

Wadding
Available in different thicknesses (weights). The type used for the projects in this book is polyester and fully washable once inside its fabric casing.

Wall plug
Use a wall plug that matches the screw size when making a wall fixing.

Stamp and small roller

Oil-based

Sanding block

Modelling clay

Suppliers

The following very kindly supplied materials and props for the projects and photography.

Ikea
Brent Park, 255 North Circular Road,
London NW10 OJQ
(Tel. 0181 451 5566)
Three-drawer chest of drawers and rug on page 9.
Wooden chair and table on page 21.
Wooden shelf units, noticeboard and large crocodile on page 35.
Wooden bed, bedside unit, lamp and wooden car on page 43.
Eight-drawer chest on page 47.
Table and chairs on page 53.
Rattan chair, table and lamp on page 57.
Rug on page 67.

Jali
Apsley House, Chartham, Canterbury,
Kent CT4 7HT
(Tel. 01227 831710)
Shaped MDF pelmet on page 9.
Shaped MDF shelf edging on page 35.
Shaped MDF wave trim on page 61.

Crown Paints
PO Box 37, Crown House, Hollins Road, Darwen,
Lancs BB3 OBG
(Tel. 01254 704951)
All the paints used for the sets and the projects came from the Crown Expressions range.

Jay-Be Furniture
Dewsbury Mills, Thornhill Road, Dewsbury,
West Yorkshire WF12 9QE
(Tel. 01924 455381)
White wrought-iron bed on page 15.

Brother Sewing Machine
Jones & Brothers, Shepley Street, Audenshaw,
Manchester M34 5JD
(Tel. 0161 330 6531)
The Star machine was used to make up all the projects that involved sewing.

Harris Paint Brushes
Stoke Prior, Bromsgrove, Worcs B60 4AE
(Tel. 01527 575441)

Blackfriars Blackboard Paint
E. Parsons & Sons, Blackfriars Road,
Bristol BS19 2DJ
(Tel. 01275 854911)
Paint used to create blackboard wall on page 61.

English Stamp Company
Sunnydown, Worth Matravers, Dorset BH19 3JP
(Tel. 01929 439117)
Playing card stamps used on page 53.
Stamp used on wooden box on page 67.

Boras fabric
4a Boardman Road, Swadlincote,
Derbyshire DE11 9DL
(Tel. 01283 550011)
Curtain, blind and window seat fabric on page 9.

Speedy Products
Speedy House, Cheltenham Street, Pendleton,
Salford M6 6WY
(Tel. 0161 737 1001)
Curtain pole on page 21 and page 53.

Lakeland Plastics
Alexandra Buildings, Windermere,
Cumbria LA23 1BQ
(Tel. 015394 88100)
Hatboxes on page 15.
Coloured basket storage system on page 61.

Haute Déco
556 Kings Road, London SW6 2DZ
(Tel. 0171 736 7171)
Coloured handles on page 47.

Index

A

anti-stain treatment, fabrics 38, 76

B

bags, PVC kit bag 30–33
balls, sports peg rail 30–33
bean bag, 'fat cat' 26, 71
beds:
   bow bed canopy 14–19
   noughts and crosses
      headboard game 42–45
   blackboard, porthole 60–65
   bow bed canopy 14–19
brackets, pelmet 13, 76
bradawls 76
brown paper 76
brushes 76–77
button pelmet 8–13

C

canopy, bow 14–17
chair, pom-pom 20–25
chalk, porthole blackboard
60–65
chests:
   eight-drawer chest 46–51
   painted and stamped toy chest
      66–69
colourwashing 49, 76
curtains:
   hold-backs 8–13
   playing card curtains 52–55
   tab-topped curtains 52
   tie-backs 52–55
cushion, pom-pom 20–25
cutting MDF 10

D

'daisy daisy' noticeboard 38–41
door knobs 23
double-ended screws 23
dowelling 76
fabric-fronted shelf units 37
drawers, eight-drawer chest
46–51
drill bits 76
drills 76
duster, starfish 64–65
duvet covers 14, 17
dyeing trimmings 24

E

eight-drawer chest 46–51
elephant pocket storage system
56–59
emulsion paint 49, 69, 76

F

fabric pens 59
fabrics:
   anti-stain treatment 38, 76
   'daisy daisy' noticeboard
      38–41
   fabric-fronted shelf units
      34–37
   selvedges 77
   tacking 41
   turning through to right side
      16
'fat cat' bean bag 26–29
felt 44
filler 76
fish pockets 64–65
French seams 19, 76
furniture:
   eight-drawer chest 46–51

painted and stamped toy chest
66–69
   pom-pom chair 20–25

G

games, noughts and crosses
headboard 42–45
glaze 76
glitter pens 59
glue 76
   spray glue 60, 76

H

handles:
   eight-drawer chest 49–51
   rope handles 69
headboard game, noughts and
crosses 42–45
hold-backs 8–13

J

jigsaws, cutting MDF 10

K

key, surfaces 76
kit bag, PVC 30–33

M

machine sewing 29
masking tape 11, 36, 76
MDF (medium density fibreboard) 76
   cutting 10
   skirting board trim 65
modelling clay 12, 76
   button pelmet 12
   sports peg rail 32

N

noticeboard, 'daisy daisy' 38–41
noughts and crosses headboard
game 42–45

O

oil-based paints 11, 22, 34, 76
oil-based varnish 77
openings, hand sewing 25

P

paint rollers 76
paintbrushes 76–77
painted and stamped toy chest
66–69
paints:
   blackboard 60
   colourwashing 49, 76
   emulsion 46, 69, 76
   oil-based 11, 22, 34, 76
   primer 11, 22, 77
   spray paints 60
   for stamping 69
   techniques 36
   top coats 10
   varnishing 23, 50–51
paper, brown 76
peg rail, sports 30–33
pelmet, button 8–13
pelmet brackets 13, 76
pens, fabric 59
pillowcases 14, 17
playing card curtains and tie-
backs 52–55
pockets:
   elephant pocket storage
      system 56–59
   porthole blackboard 63
polystyrene balls 26, 29

polyurethane varnish 23, 77
pom-pom chair 20-25
porthole blackboard 60-65
primer 11, 22, 77
PVC:
    fabric-fronted shelf units
    34-37
    PVC kit bag 30-33

R
rollers, paint 76
rope 33
rope handles 69

S
sanding blocks 77
sandpaper 22

satin-finish paints 22
screws, double-ended 23
seams:
    French 19, 76
    machine sewing 55
selvedges 77
shelf units, fabric-fronted 34-37
skirting board, MDF trim 65
slipstitch 25, 77
sports peg rail 30-33
spray paints 60
stains, anti-stain treatment 40
stamping 77
    toy chest 66-69
staple guns 77
starfish duster 64-65
stitches, slipstitch 25, 77
storage:
    eight-drawer chest 46-51

elephant pocket storage
system 56-59
fabric-fronted shelf units
34-37
painted and stamped toy
chest 66-69
sports peg rail 30-33

T
tab-topped curtains 52
tacks 37, 41, 77
templates 70-75
tie-backs, playing card 52-55
toy chest, painted and stamped
66-69
trimmings:
    dyeing 24
    MDF 65

V
varnishes 23, 51, 77
Velcro 36, 42, 77

W
wadding 77
    'daisy daisy' noticeboard 40
    playing card curtains 55
wall plugs 77
windows:
    button pelmet 8-13
    playing card curtains and tie-
    backs 52-55
wood:
    colourwashing 49
    cutting MDF 10
    priming 11, 22, 77